Ash Dickinson has been full-time as a poet since 2008. He is slam champion, including Edinburgh, Scotland and BBC Radio. He has per  USA, Spain, Jordan, the Czech Republic countless shows and festivals through demand to run writing workshops in prisons and with writing groups. His deb was the very first title published by Burning Eye Books. His second major collection, *Strange Keys*, also released by Burning Eye, came out in 2016. A collection for younger years, *Show Cats In Transit*, came out in 2019.

FOR THE POETRY VICTOR,
THE SPOILS...
REMEMBER WHAT IT IS
TO FLY...
HAPPY READING!

ASH

Instructions for Outlaws

Ash Dickinson

Burning Eye

BurningEyeBooks
Never Knowingly
Mainstream

This edition published by Burning Eye Books 2022

www.burningeye.co.uk

@burningeyebooks

Burning Eye Books

15 West Hill, Portishead, BS20 6LG

ISBN 978-1-913958-23-7

Instructions for Outlaws

CONTENTS

In Prison	9
Self-Absorbent	10
I Don't Have a Chair in the House	12
Page Against the Machine	13
Goosanders	15
Shadorma Intermission I	16
Watch-Bear of the Family Crest	17
Under the Pads	20
A Father Explains the Meaning of Life to His Plankton Offspring	22
Tungsten in the Crosshairs	24
Nonet Intermission I	27
I Was a Teenage Axl Rose	28
Another Woman	31
Mango, the Reading Retriever	32
Hipsters Ruined Beards	33
Shadorma Intermission II	36
Crime Scenes	37
Kestrel	39
In the Moon	41
Eleven Hotdogs	43
Pearlfisher	45
Nonet Intermission II	47
21st Century Boy II	48
D'ough	49
Spatchcocked Gull	51
Run for No Reason	53
Both Ends of a Cracker	55
Drinking in Reverse	56
Haiku Intermission	58
In an Octopus's Betting Syndicate Under the Sea	59

A Thousand Dead Canaries 60
44,000 Grams of Pure H2O 61
Two and a Half Chords 64
Twenty-Five on Twenty-Five 66
Shadorma Intermission III 68
Good Morning Vitamin 69
This Poem 72
An American Beer Company Presents: The Royal Mile 73
My Girl, the Wasp Tormentor 75
Bowl Cut 77
Nonet Intermission III 80
No Good at Accents 81
Pommel Tapir 83
I Wasn't Born 84
Unfree Verse 86
Radio Emo 88
Americana 89
Shadorma Intermission IV 91
Freshers' Week 92
Fenland Infidelity 93
A Corvid Audience 94
Fox Fishing 97
Diaries: Instructions for Outlaws 100

IN PRISON

it didn't feel like criticism
of my writing prompts
he simply said he preferred to freestyle

incarcerated, I understood
the paper was another cage
not for him the page's way
of herding thoughts' wayward birds
in some lives there are already too many rules
it was as though his words lost height
on that ride from mind to pen to sheet
surrendered their freedom

he sat up a little in his chair
closed his eyes, summoned thunder
began to spit out bars

and when he'd spat out bars
he spat out prison walls, the prison guards
every knockdown, every lockdown
all his lifeblood ran in that rhythm

and when finally he came up for breath
he'd soared right out that prison, a free man

SELF-ABSORBENT

my skin isn't waterproof
it is made of a fibre
similar to cotton

want proof? leave me out in a thunderplump
see me transformed into someone
who's survived a parachute jump   without a parachute
falling   falling   splat, spread flat
wrapped in my own tarpaulin

in sodden bags-for-life bags of arms
bags of back and bags of chest, gripped
in sodden tote bag hands
I limp-drag that squelchy sack back home
like an accidentally shot hunting buddy
to lie on a radiator once again
like a pampered cat
until the reservoir drains

the recovery time for a bath
is vast; pre-work, I must set an alarm
four hours early. drying
time is reduced in summer months
when I elbow the lizards for room
on a flat rock by the back door
fill every crevice with my form
point its horror at a celestial body
ninety million miles away
and crinkle-dry like an error-washed lottery ticket

I'm not entirely permeable
open season for microorganisms
my top layer lets everything through
but the hypodermis is a seawall
my organs, like yours, are unadventurous shut-ins

holidaying indoors
while my outer skin disperses
pining for the coast

one day I hope to meet an understanding woman
open to a move to Death Valley
a thrill-seeker maybe, girlish and giddy
white water rafting my knee
to Shangri-La   to where Christ the Redeemer
stands open-armed
as the skies cave in

she will know me like fingerprints
and when the rains relent
she will come back to me   and stay
comfortable in my skin

I DON'T HAVE A CHAIR IN THE HOUSE

I don't have a chair in the house
I don't like to sit
I haven't sat since the mid-eighties
it's not just lazy, it's bad for posture
I don't have furniture, I eat standing up
I burn calories faster

you don't own a TV, you say?
I don't have walls
I've been sans-wall since '98
you get a wall, a day later
you've ninety pictures
four dozen mirrors
if I need to see my reflection
I'll stare into the teeth of a prosperous friend
eyes might be windows to the soul
but 21st-century pegs are the disco balls

people talk about decluttering
downsizing, adopting a Buddhist ethos
I'm down to three bathrooms, they'll say, two waffle makers –
I don't own a floor, haven't had a floor
since before I had a wall
it's the inconvenience – floors demand stuff
they need carpeting, they need vacuuming
                    floors / need / furniture
and I don't own a chair
I don't like to sit

want to live more minimalist?
you've got to commit

PAGE AGAINST THE MACHINE

your body can be rebuilt
every artery, every sinew
whatever's in you
replicated and improved, refitted glands
your heart can pulse like Iron Man's
but it won't be filled with orchids, or kids' stories
vignettes of moments, elegiac movements
that can break your heart
or make you laugh out loud
I wondered lonely as the cloud
that floats on high
storing and accessing data

infinite monkey theorem states
you sit a chimp at a keyboard for eternity
eventually it will write something worthwhile
it's similar to Dan Brown theorem
but the keyboard itself?
a sentient being, existentialism?
fears of rusting and a bust caps lock?
games consoles with souls?
The Love Song of J Alfred Xbox?

when your bank account
is stripped in seconds, money a construct
digits in a database, tellers mere screens rebooting
when fear and panic lead to looting
when we all head to the UK's only store –
the Amazon repository, located in what was Luton
when we bang on its Castle Grayskull gates
useless debit cards clutched in impotent fists
screaming for electronics that can bathe and change us
don't despair, there's more currency in your library card
more lasting riches in the pages of bards

when animals are extinct
and eighties-obsessed machines
have built us K9 and odd tin owls
from the Harry Hamlin *Clash of the Titans*
everything we displaced, predated
recreated to keep us sedated
kittens made from wire wool, bits of old PlayStations
where there is need for pets, there is need for poets
to write of nature, evoke a future
transport us across time – the Bardis
unicorns exist   because they exist in us

and when you're jobsolete, your trade taken by motors
and gears, food servers replaced by food-servers
gone the soldiers, the farmers, the pharmacists
the teachers, the cleaners, the scientists
when human egg chambers stretch across the Norfolk Broads
when toasters are our overlords
when you're controlled by your phone   uh-oh, too late
there will be all the more need for poets
find an alcove, pour out your thoughts
scrawl *DOWN WITH THE MACHINES* caps and all
if you're caught – turn your captor off at the wall
scramble its signals with metaphor
rage against the machine
say its mother was a SodaStream
interface? – in your face!

can't recall when you were last outside
your whole life delivered, friends online
it's fine
not heard a friendly voice in weeks
talking to yourself just to hear speech
write the human condition—
it's what separates man
          from beeps

GOOSANDERS

the males away on a Norwegian stag
we found the female goosanders'
own aftermath, wild

preposterous tufts, no signs
of curling irons or straighteners
slept-in-their-clothes Rod Stewart tribute acts

a gaggle of starlets going out for fags
without lippy, unconcerned that coot
in the bushes might be paparazzi

the morning after the night before
the sun a runny egg, kippers for dippers

an empty bottle of prosecco bobs past
another two on the bank, a cache

hand-me-down brioche rebuffed
they're out for lunch, gone fishing
bottoms up

SHADORMA INTERMISSION I

he grew veg
otherworldly stuff
huge rocket
moon-size peas
onion rings of Saturn. one
giant leek for man

nerve agent
deployed. agents' nerve
not lost on
sleepy town
that awakes slowly to news
if it wakes at all

fill your face
a finger buffet
(see thumbnails)
hand parcels
canape metacarpals
knuckle sandwiches

WATCH-BEAR OF THE FAMILY CREST

I'd always known I was a bear; nothing
was just right. my parents thought
my appetite healthy, but what growing boy
desires half a ton of fish fingers a day?

in childhood photos, I am rarely
without a proto-onesie
of thick brown fur
my grizzling was a low growl

in the playground, friends
would be Han Solo and BA Baracus
and Spider-Man
I was Bungle
from *Rainbow*

toddlers don't fall into zoo enclosures
it's force – apes and wolves caged in boys and girls
driven by instinct, they must climb in

first time I saw a grizzly, I shouted 'Daddy!'
couldn't help it, it roared out of me
the daddy I arrived with ran to me
he can't hurt you, he said, reassuringly
shaking and sobbing in his arms
I saw Karhu that day, I saw Ursa Major

he took me for an ice cream to calm me down
to see the macaws, the llamas, the petting farm
nothing that could frighten me
but at the gift shop I asked for a plastic bear mask
I wore it round the house, to and from each class
wore it until the elastic snapped
then got replaced, snapped then got replaced

how does one be a bear?
some things were innate
otherwise, as with most my age
TV assumed role of teacher and sage

from *Gentle Ben*
I understood I'd enjoy
snaking through swamps
on a motorised throne

from *The Jungle Book*
I learnt what fruits are safe to consume
and that I must sing, often –
'The Bare Necessities'
became my anthem
my 'All You Need Is Love'

at the first opportunity
I joined the Cubs
I didn't care for the den meets
and washing people's cars
but in the woods I was home
I chased rabbits with a throaty roar
explored for prickly pears
and pawpaws among the pinecones
the other kids left me alone
true cubs they weren't

imagine growing up
knowing you're not who you are
I went through adolescence
like any youngster who knows
they're really a bear –
I lied, mostly to myself
went to the discos
the playing fields, snuck honey
into my cider at the park
I never rode a bicycle –

couldn't rid my mind
of captive brethren, pitiful in hats
the old circus photographs
but I took to water
like a supermarket trolley

every opportunity I'd visit the zoo
in her confidence, the keeper
at the polar enclosure disclosed
her spirit animal had long been the bear
I would picture her there after hours
totemically positioning one atop another
I at the head, watch-bear of the family crest
carved snout, broad paws, eyes
fixed beyond grey city walls
to dense, verdant pines of the north
and there, where the paternal Rockies jut
I'd shed my skin at the edge of an ice blue lake
and stride in   barefoot

UNDER THE PADS

it's buried
under the jersey
under the pads
under the skin

hidden, concealed
weakened and broken
and healed, a flag
on the field of play
a ridge of magnetism
luring in 300-pound bloodhounds
chum for every defensive lineman

x marks the tissue
standard issue

the locker room
is a campaign map
here you can read a man
like braille, trace
the aftermath
of titanic clashes
visible lines
of scrimmage

sat, bench-pressed
half-undressed
masses of muscle, sweat
crossing battlelines
scars as decoration
as declaration, fresh
and knuckled
as Superbowl rings

unraised skin
raises suspicion
the unblemished
anyone for tennis
doesn't wash here
the drafted ducker
of incoming tackles
you need to know
someone has your back
they need to have done
the hard yards

squared up
to monstrous brutes
blocking routes
to first downs, gone in
high and hard, last ditch
rupturing earth
skin like ripped turf
stitched up
like the game ball
hauled to your feet
by teammates
your impact
on the play mostly unseen
in the bleachers, on screen
to others the headlines
your effect, their glory
on the sidelines, the high-fives
tell a different story

under the pads
under the scars
beneath the muscle –
blood and heart, part and parcel

A FATHER EXPLAINS THE MEANING OF LIFE TO HIS PLANKTON OFFSPRING

Dad, a couple of clownfish at school were taunting me. They said I don't belong to a phylogenetic or taxonomic classification and so, being defined essentially as an ecological niche, I'm a stupidface.

Son, now listen to me. We are the most important organisms in the entire ocean. Without us there would be no herring, no shark, no blue whale. No clownfish.

But they said we're food. Is that right? If so, we're no better than a Coco Pop.

We're a superfood, son.

Like quinoa?

Better than quinoa, son. We're the food the whole sea depends upon. Indeed, our importance isn't bound by shores or tide. Without us there'd be nothing.

But why, Dad? Why must we give ourselves so others can live? Are our lives less important?

It's called the food chain, son. Every living thing plays its part. We're not only a fundamental cog in the process; we're also its catalyst. We're numero uno. Not only are we the primary food source, but we help to produce 50% of the world's oxygen. Without our initial impact, all life would essentially collapse.

But what if it was a food wall? What if, instead of eating us, all us plankton and all the fish and all the dolphins and all the whales just hung out instead and danced and played ping-pong?

But what would the fish and the dolphins and the whales eat, son? If not us or the fish that eat us, they'd all die out. All that would be left is plankton.

So, if we didn't allow ourselves to be eaten, Dad, we'd rule the world?

...er, yes... son... we'd rule the world...

TUNGSTEN IN THE CROSSHAIRS

found an elephant skull
at the foot of the garden
beyond the radishes and cabbages
a bull male, disembodied, discarded
stripped of flesh and bulk
a bleach-white bulb
so I dug a deep hole – *to plant*
an elephant

pack terra firma firmly
over pachyderm and pat
water liberally – torrents
that relieve the Serengeti
of its aridity give life to
parched mammalian bone

poachers came by increasingly
trampled the hydrangeas
unsettled the rockery
rested rifles against the trunk
of a gnarled oak
struck matches against its skin
surveyed the shoots emerging
from ripening earth as they smoked
rows and rows of carrot tails
embryonic trunked fronts
waiting on a harvest
of elephants
for unbroken days of sun

I let them roam, competitors
for a prize marrow
watched them salivate, seeing
each elephant grow
into a potential best in show

they called my garden *L'Eden Blanc*
sensed, heady as blossom
a downpour to end all drought
but these tusks would not be ivory
these tusks were tungsten

I righted the panda, added a wider diet
lust to its lustre; sometimes nature
needs a helping hand, to take a stand
or bat away the death-grip of man

the look on the face
of the first poacher to notice!
he tapped, stunned, the arm of the man closest
pointed to the glint of gun-metal
aimed at his slight, sunken chest
sixty barrels breaking topsoil
shanty towns packed up in minutes
I spent the next two hours
combing out footprints
collecting up cigarette butts
from the gazebo

one terrible morning
I'd come to see tungsten
was coveted elsewhere – darts players
woken by foreboding jangling –
Bobby George's bling
rattling by my window –
I pulled back the curtain
to see Michael van Gerwen
aiming a blunderbuss at the herd
his accuracy, tragically, unerring

I dressed, heavy-hearted
hauled my body down the hall
past vast aquaria of polar bears
stopping at the last, in order

to watch two females force water
through gills, turn
and spin like gymnasts
loitered until my spirits lifted nearly new
then turned on my heel, spun like them
began work on elephants: mark II

NONET INTERMISSION I

reports of canine dysmorphia
continue to dog Crufts. boxers
well below their fighting weight
bulimic bichon frise
in their tracks. pressure
to look the best
in show. com-
paring
hounds

they argued for miles then fell silent
at the turnoff to Aylesbury
the brewer's droop of the south
accusations raw, thick
freshener tree felled, limp
(avoided) eyes
on gear stick
standing
proud

I WAS A TEENAGE AXL ROSE

I was a teenage Axl Rose
one in a million in matte photos
jacket patched 'Paradise City'
bandana (obligatory). observe
the hair grow   to mirror his
(pre-cornrows)
short back and sides snarl
(the It's So Easy intro)
extending to full-blown November Rain solo
I longed for it
down to my toes
anything goes

metalled to the hilt
pining for a kilt
and to wear my underwear outside
I was a teenage Axl Rose
but mine was an upbringing built
on the bourgeois, where only arias
classed as singing; for supper –
foie gras, free-range chicken
bon appétit for destruction
an insular white picket fence close
where alfresco teeny-tiny shorts
would set the tweed set to stare, arrythmia
to flare / cause frantic calls
for long white coats

sure, my squabbles with authority
were minor, my tattoos rub-on
or hand-drawn with eyeliner
skull tats that would yield
to a licked thumb or hot bath
I was a teenage Axl Rose
no police-baiting, dog-hating

crowd-inciting, fist-fighting
I'd get up about eleven
I'd go to bed around nine   nine thirty
if Mum was feeling generous
or *Challenge Anneka* was on
I once hitchhiked to Beeston

underage and under illusion
I was a teenage Axl Rose
scouting off-licences for Night Train
making do with Lambrini, something pink
drink a third down the park then throw up
there's rock-'n'-roll heroism
in puking up your guts
I ain't no Bon Scott but
that's a whole lotta rosé to me

I was the black sheep
late every lunch date
making others wait
for two hours   more
(forgoing all but dessert)
two spoonfuls – I'd wig out
call the ice cream 'too cold'
flip the bowl

bring up the house lights
drop the curtain
fourteen years old
holder of a rage
I was certain
could only be understood
by one other person
I was a teenage Axl Rose

odd then to be remodelled by grunge
my kilt fixation expunged
by flannel shirts, Ten, Dirt

my mate Gareth – Slash to my Axl –
started wearing olive-green Farahs
polo shirts of a delicate pastel
artistic differences
he took up with Kylie
I headed for Seattle

now you can buy GNR
T-shirts at Primark   in toddler sizes
the band's official site advertises
woollens with holiday slogans
claims to danger unspun, bogus
they are the soft and safe band
that soft and safe boy merited
choreographed rebellion in a clean-nose age
corporate cleaned-up old-hit shows
reunited for the money, throw
some half-remembered pose
they know this cheque
(it once lived down on Melrose)
that Coma swagger comatose
heritage and gone to hell
farewell – and yowza! – teenage Axl Rose

ANOTHER WOMAN

caught him looking at pictures of her
again. young, flippant beauty
eclipsing the photography
limbs limber and lissom, lines
smudged into her lineless face
from hungrily insistent thumbs

how do I compete with that?
twenty-six years younger, tiny flat tummy
unstretched from another surefire fix
no grey has yet weathered her hair
that summery stare burning up
the camera, full of vigour
what does she know
of disappointment?

rumbled, he fumbles the shot
I blunder out there, fast up the stairs
slam the spare room door behind me

I know what's coming

'but it's you, darling,' he shouts again
from the foot of the stairs

holding on to an image
of another woman

MANGO, THE READING RETRIEVER

Mango, the reading retriever
is read to by primary pupils
to improve literacy
it has worked
she is now the most well-read canine
in the country

with a reading age of twelve
(which in dog years is seventy-seven)
she laps up complex sentence structure –
to her, a book is worth any bone from any butcher
this precociousness
eventually led to her enrolment in class
in no time, she rose to be Head Girl

when she dreams, she dreams
of pea-green boats, fields of rabbits
sent scattering as she runs to sand
wet as her nose, to search the horizon
for Robinson Crusoe, go
where the wild things go, go
to meet the mouse that knows the Gruffalo

when she whimpers, front leg a-twitch
she has found lost treasure
that attracts four children
the whole world ahead of them
an endless summer opening up
like the unimaginable pleasure
that awaits you in a book

HIPSTERS RUINED BEARDS

Once upon a time I was one of only three people in the UK to have a beard. Noel Edmonds and a strongman were the others. If you're thinking, hang on, I've had a beard for forty years, you haven't; it's shadow.

My beard would stop traffic, halt planes in mid-flight. I've witnessed terrifying men, upon seeing my beautifully bushy face, break down and sob like infants, claw nearly to the bone their infertile jowls. On occasions, my beard would be big and burly like the Black Forest, like Chuck Norris; other times dangerously streamlined, like a well-kempt chin shark. Throughout the nineties, it was there – an ever-dependable retriever of the lower face.

Many tried to imitate. I watched a man at a Cranberries gig affix a clutch of twigs to his jawline with gaffer tape. My newsagent favoured lashings of Crayola. Help was at hand, however. Beard transplants became possible on the NHS. I myself took to carrying a Beard Donor Card certifying I would donate my facial hair so someone could have beard-life after I was gone. It was the least I could do. I'd known the pain close to home – my own cousin was perilously clean-shaven for months, awaiting delivery of a handlebar moustache.

Alternative remedies flooded the market. As a young buck, impatiently awaiting the full flush of beard maturity, I cultivated a moustache of bees. (NB: a full beard of bees requires round-the-clock upkeep. If you can only get your hands on hornets, don't despair – they are an entirely acceptable substitute and a decent halfway house for the beard beginner with designs on sculpting a bee goatee or, eventually, a fully formed facial fuzz of wasps.)

I'm straying from the Van Dyke of my argument. Three people in the UK had real, actual beards. For years. Then the hipster arrived. Overnight, the world groaned under the weight of its whiskers. There were beards everywhere – on men, children, women, on animals. The Cookie Duster. The Parisian Throat-Stroker. The Thigh Tingler. The

Egyptian Nose Combover. The shaving of the entire face, save for one individual hair grown a foot and a half long from just   there.

My beard lost its uniqueness – and I my identity. I was subsumed in a maelstrom of mainstream. Bird of paradise turned town pigeon. I was tarred as hipster, feathered. In cafés, attendants would bring my girlfriend and her friends coffee in nice cups, then serve mine in a plimsoll decorated with cuttings of the cast of *Last of the Summer Wine*. I would be stopped on the street and asked to recommend gins. People I vaguely knew at work – now all bearded – would invite me bicycling, followed by 'posh eggs'. I came to believe *hipster* derived from the trousers; all I saw, everywhere, were asses.

Throughout many sleep-ravaged nights, I contemplated shaving off the beard – but have you ever stared at a wall that previously held a masterpiece? I couldn't bear the thought of the pasty flock of my under-face.

Time is a fickle master – I simply needed to ride it out. To speed its end, I embraced all hipster customs, shone a light on them, exaggerated them for their lunacy. The irony was exhausting. I did get to flaunt my musical knowledge, sneer at the saps who thought TV on the Radio peaked with their debut. Hipster porridge was better than mine – why had I never thought to mix in quinoa and porcini mushrooms, then top it off with a thimble?

Before long I was waxing and sculpting my facial hair into elaborate shapes and taking Polaroids of it. On Instagram, I entitled one *The Hanging Gardens of Babylon*. My mind was gone. My beard had grown foot-long tentacles that had slithered down my ear canal and perforated my brain. I would spend all night in the pub talking about my beard, whilst stroking it like the cat of a supervillain. I both loved and loathed every other beard I saw. I was in competition – and I was in awe. I was a pageant hopeful, smiling and hugging everyone, while secretly wishing all would fall.

I thought of the bewigged gentlemen of the 18th century. The trickle
down from regent and nobility. The ubiquity. How hard to stand out,
among the perfumed candyfloss, the apers and charlatans. If my own
beard hadn't been so pioneering? If it hadn't resembled chinstrap
gold…? I knew I must shoulder some of the blame. This is the face
that spawned a million copyists. Undeniably that knowledge took
away some of the gloss. I was the Chuck Berry that begat Maroon 5.
The Logie Baird that gave us *Love Island*.

Of course, you're reading this in 2059; you know the hipster perished.
Look down at your ankles; you're almost certainly wearing flares.
Every other person you know is named Ash. You probably are now.
You're at your fourth spoken word event of the week at your town's
purpose-built poetry enormodome. Your hair has grown. This might
be the day you came on board. Welcome, you'll have a terrific time.
We make the world in our own image. You were busy, though,

so you appropriated mine.

SHADORMA INTERMISSION II

bright magpie
only nonmammal
to know its
own image
one for sorrow no more, they've
discovered selfies

fire crews free
next generation
skinned by swings
made for tots
outdone. outfoxed. China spies
walkover. tick… tock…

children named
after a city
Paris, Ri-
o… Sydney?
a trend of the times, I told
my firstborn, Brussels

CRIME SCENES

ten minutes late, we ghost in at the back
detective inspector (retired)
deconstructing crime scenes
budding crime writers
scribbling in their Moleskines

we're Bonnie and Clyde
nonchalant, no paper, no pen
making no notes, taking it all in
instructions for outlaws

she nods towards the mightiest weapon
on a table, if required
good girl, eyes wide
DI, clothed by his wife, in the midst
of forensic analysis, seized knickers
they all jot it down

there's more honesty in committing crime than writing it
look around the room – fantasists and the cowardly
you couldn't be a travel writer and never go anywhere

how far would you carry a child's dead body?
the old boys asks – rhetorical? a trap?
my girl and I trade glances, we know this one
we could take it from here

incident pattern analysis, precursors leading to suspects
telephone records, psychological profiling
open questions – poor buggers don't stand a chance

this is our thirty-eighth of these
we've seen this guy three times
he smiled our way, offered us a biscuit at the break
we abducted a kid after his last one
changed our modus operandi, swayed by a case study

he reaches the part about bodies cemented into houses
she gives my knee a little squeeze, we like this bit
you can't lay a price on nights like these
I holster my chin into her shoulder blade
shut my eyes a little, slip away
thirty people here hoping to make crime pay
they're listening to the wrong guy

KESTREL

suspended, a static kite
feathers making minor
adjustments, eyesight
sharp and focused
on imperceptible movements
in grass, wild as uncut hair

joggers, many new to it
store folds still in their cotton
pass at a safe distance
(we're all out on our allotted
one exercise of the day)
couples with dogs
those alone   like me

no one else's eyes
seem to be
on that same patch of sky
mesmerised

when we could still travel freely
and my work took me
to Reading or Wycombe
there'd be actual kites
urban pterodactyls
gold-eyed winged lions
wrought of menace, precision
gilded upon leaden skies
populous as pigeons

I've thought to stop pedestrians
share gawped fortune, only to stop short
what might he point at next – a leaf? soil?
water forming a puddle? his own breath?

twenty-three hours a day quarantined
might change all that. to be out
in nature, buoyant. to go up
to a stranger for a chat

pushing forward
into the headwinds
going nowhere
in paused isolation
suspended animation
life up in the air

IN THE MOON

what if the moon were hollow
like a ping-pong ball
and you could crack its surface
with a fingernail, make a hole
big enough to insert your fist
your wrist, your elbow – more so
your shoulder, your face, your torso
until nothing/ holds/ you
and you fall/ straight/ through
fall
and fall
fall
the moon has a diameter
of 2,159 miles
fall
and fall
fall
its gravity is much less than the Earth's
fall
and fall
fall
into all
that empty space, the colossal
nothingness between poles

you'd eventually come to rest
on its inner surface
roll like a marble
back and forth
along the jawbone
of its wide white face
a pea sealed inside a balloon

you might run the moon
like a hamster ball

unmoor its orbital brakes
pedal hard until it rotates
every side, every phase
imagine outrunning the sun
joyriding deeper and deeper
into outer space

here, on Earth, on clear nights
the moon, full and glowing
with collected light; turn
an ear… listen for sound
its traveller's tune
the trapped tap-tap-tap
the feet that beat 'Clair de Lune'
the restless rhythms
of the man in the moon

ELEVEN HOTDOGS

I'd advised the wife
to rip up the invite
but she pressed my good shirt
and muttered darkly of responsibilities
of divorce. we've been here before
of course, many times:
The Barbecue
hell in microcosm

I open a beer and conversation
with Tony, but his eyes
and thirty more
our mushed-up banana minds
are directed
towards some three-year-old
engaged in typically three-year-old things

he isn't my kid
he doesn't belong
to twenty-eight of us here
at three, he doesn't appear
to be a world-class gymnast
or multifaceted entertainer
he's textbook

there's more distraction
captivation
in the fruit bowl
the manicured surrounds
in the summer blouses
and frankly between my mucky toes

we're not in the presence of Christ
as far as I can ascertain
I just want to drink

and eat eleven hotdogs
and engage in adult conversation

if I'd known this
was a kid's party
I'd have brought a gift
and left room for jelly

and where the hell is my goody bag?

PEARLFISHER

they tethered you like an animal
a beast of burden; they couldn't fathom
your depths

cast you off again to that cold
and lonely sea, to search the shallows
for oyster treasure

they – drinking, laughing, you on a string
you – topless, silent, a slip of a thing
a shadow, a shape   shimmering
through crystalline depths
from on deck, they look down on you
consider your soul
worthless   your body monetised
a dive for a dive   for a dive

                              to never imagine
to live a life of dismal pragmatism
to not see pearl, only price, shut off
to something soft and smooth
and sparkling sheen, the sea
a snatched purse

buckled over bow, sweat beading
confused brows, dropping
to the ripples like buckshot rain
closest to water, to you, they came

tragic   to only grasp wonder
when it's far under and gone forever
gone to where light doesn't travel, hair
forming coral, swaying in prettied ribbons

they never understand every dive
took a little longer, took you a little further

didn't notice your tanned skin turn to scales
tiny iridescent tiles that gemmed in sunlight
as you opened like a shuttered shell

                                    they lost sight of you
in that patch of sea they thought you'd be
but weren't   rope coming up easily, empty
no more pearls for swine

the stars as instruments
navigational points
never tender light
jewelling the surface
like vast schools
of undredged silver fish

          you have taken the stars
left them, dark
rudderless
but what illimitable sky
to cast the mind across
what bottomless depths
no one told the stars they're dead

starboard, a star jump, five points
of light, halo-haired and branching limbs
a glimpse of bare sole kicking up foam
the etherealness of a feather, of a fin

NONET INTERMISSION II

famed Chesterfield architect, plans leant
on immaculate construction
accidental pinnacle
town steeple steeped in myth
he wasn't crooked
was the wood, lead
to that peak
luck's in-
spired

I met my wife on eharmony
we wanted the same thing – an ex
-tramarital affair. fair
enough – we'd grown distant
four hours online
my top match, natch
upstairs on
her lap
top

21ST CENTURY BOY II

I'm watching my intake, taking protein shakes
lifting weights, I'm getting healthy
I start each day with a reassuring selfie
I can go out with a woman and outlast her shopping
six hours not close to dropping
stopping for food, we both choose the lighter option
I'm happy with soy
I'm a 21st century boy

I've lost my father's skills and craft
I know nothing about plumbing
– there are professionals for that
I can't change a fuse
but I do like a jaunty hat
I'm up with the news
I know birthdays, I'm not afraid to weep
it's not a weakness
nor is the whiteness of my teeth
the abs I flaunt along the beach
I hunt the high street for outerwear, gather
enough product for statement hair
my beard has 10,000 followers on Instagram
I'm a 21st century man

think sweat man's one true scent?
guys' clothing should be at all times unobtrusive
and preferably flecked with dry cement? – experiment
think outside the Boxfresh   think Bowie
my gender won't limit me
I can be whatever I want to be
open up, show fragility
get my heart broken
show emotions, insecurity
and I can write poetry
twenty
            first century
                    boy

D'OUGH

are you sitting comfortably?
they've got all your childhood favourites
advertising products; there's nothing
like nostalgia to shift the units
Scooby-Dooby-Doo, where are you?
you've got some home insurance to sell now
load up the van, you're working for The Man
all your high ideals have gone to hell now
Shaggy would never have consented to this...
contents insurance? he's a hippie –
they eschew possessions
the Halifax must have something on him –
incriminating pictures of nights out
in straight-legged trousers
his parents tied up and gagged in an abandoned funfair

you want a corporate shill, you create one –
Maurice, the Cashback Llama
APR Variable, the wisecracking squirrel
draft in Tony the Tiger – he's industry
a yes-man: Tony the Tie-Guy
fixed-rate mortgages? they're grrrrrrreat!
don't co-opt *Rainbow* into selling pizza
oh, Geoffrey, how much of this crust do we get?
ooh, yes, Geoffrey, I feel sick. zip it
The Flintstones? there were no cave paintings
for Poundland. mammoth savings at the carpet tar-pit
Yabba. Dabba. Don't
Russian meerkats? they're stone cold product
simples / as that
they're not beloved characters of yore
their innocence sold into capitalism
Lady Penelope coerced into a new mission
up in the air / Thunderbirds are Go
Compare. had an accident that wasn't your fault?

asks Bagpuss. no
Churchill the nodding dog? ohhhh yes
that don panda racketeering cream-filled 'bisquits'?
preposterous but yes
Chewie as the face of M&S? no
there is nothing sacrosanct that can't be used
to sell a bank/ a bread/ in-play betting/ a meal for two
two-ply toilet roll and Winnie-the-Pooh
the closer it is to your heart, the closer it is to your wallet
just leave Top Cat out of it

now SpongeBob won't put on his square pants
unless they come with a Nike swoosh
and Buzz Lightyear is flying to you
To infinity and B&Q!
Pikachu won't get out of bed
for less than 10,000 a day from Betfred
your childhood can be yours again
every fifteen minutes of every day
but it comes subliminally and at a price
when you can't make the repayments on your home
and the repo van is drawing close
your family, chilled to the bone
sleeping in the car, wrapped up in their coats
remember Porky the Pig sold you that loan
th-th-th-that's all folks

SPATCHCOCKED GULL

spatchcocked gull
phlegmatic stare
took a people-carrier
to put it there
soften cruel eyes
a mocking beak
flattened like origami sheets
no innards outwards
or splayed blood
pop it back to life
with the right fold
crease wing (fig. 1)
smooth crumpled spine
reverse-fold its tail
until all bird aligns

I've no need for swan napkins
cheap paper perfunctory
if I have folk over for tea
their place is surveyed
by road-killed ravens
rebuilt herons, a gannet
eat up quick, I'll say
before the pigeons get it

ancient Japanese legend has it
one who folds a thousand cranes
has a wish granted by the gods
– I've 991 more to go

on that day, I'll clap my hands
and every pair of wings will beat
mob windows and doors, soar
from nests of tables and floors
rumble down the hallway
to be more sky than sky

agape at the front gate
fleshed of feather, my bones light
I too will reanimate
remember what it is to fly

RUN FOR NO REASON

when did you last run
for no reason?
felt the compulsion
to break into a sprint
the propulsion, not in
the park or the gym
but on the street
push off from toes
in shoes not fit for purpose
and just go
because you wanted to
because you must

as a kid, I ran everywhere
I never once walked up stairs
the world couldn't come to me quick enough
shopping errands took minutes
Mum, silently exasperated
hoping for longer peace
but I was on wheels, naturally aspirated
Cram, Ovett at my heels, Coe
a middle-distance runner
beating all comers, a stone skimming
the sun-bleached streets of Sillitoe

the day after my fourteenth birthday
I – and a few hundred others – ran round
the pitch at Notts County's ground
with Jimmy Savile (true story)
thinking back, were we running with him
                              or away from him?

at twenty-one
I had half-marathon aspirations
in the build-up, the furthest I'd run

consecutively was six miles
chased across scrubland
by a cuckolded friend
lethargy and procrastination
kicked in, nights out
I lacked the discipline
should've met up with his girlfriend again
to help with the training

at twenty-six I raced a Norwegian
round a tree and back at a camel farm
hours after climbing Uluru – bad juju
I took a tumble in five-dollar trainers
broke my radius (gravel is my nemesis)
six screws in my arm and a metal plate
hole in my favourite jeans, and worse –
I lost the race

latterly I've run
for buses, flights, trains
I've run away from relationships
one night in Honolulu someone crossed
a deserted backstreet to my side
for directions, he said
but I got a weird vibe – fight or flight
and I bolted
at gigs, I might run over
bar tabs I might run up
I've been run down
and I've run out of luck
but I never think to widen my stride
aim at a point on the horizon
or, better, at nothing – and just go

if you can fill the unforgiving minute
with sixty seconds' worth of distance run
yours is the Earth and everything that's in it
and – which is more – you'll be fit

BOTH ENDS OF A CRACKER

the obligatory Christmas ad – mum, dad
and a cast of thousands, crowded
together from different houses
tipsy auntie, neighbours, grandkids
party hats, sherry, pigs in blankets

this year those ads might need
to be more considerate, realistic
not every Christmas Day is as depicted –
an extended table epic
as you sit alone or in your bubble
this December 25th, gripping both
ends of a cracker, in need
of a lift, short on gifts, laughter

and those usual ads come taunting
on the telly, pullback shots
of a huge, perfect family – remember
this year's scenario
is every year's scenario
for far too many

DRINKING IN REVERSE

burst capillaries disperse, return to source
a shot nose goes claret to rosé, unfills
off the sauce, stilled distilleries, shaky fists
rewind from stunned lips. shouted words
swallowed, unheard, unslurred
unpickled organs, unburdened limbs
stretch   elastic, the NHS ungroans
hospital beds – empty as doorways
sleeping bags unzipped, cider
unsipped, returned, unbought
glum barflies, wings unclipped, soar
like crows to happy homes
mental health reforming, spent memory returning
sozzled sops, the spell of proof broken
sick street smells lifting. cops
twiddle thumbs through Alcopop-less 90s
80s, 70 shillings unspent. devoted teetotalists
unthrown spousal hits, never-was thugs
unhacked, unstitched, the drink undone
sixties still swing, it's the fashion
something less for rations to stretch
stiff upper lips not searching
for the drop, an escape from something
thirties speakeasies open and close
back channels dismantled, unbuilt
bad distillers bootleg it to the hills
blind pigs see again

America took against drink
and the ripples spread across the pond
in 1922, in Chiswick, the first cask
is tipped down the sink, toodle-pip
bottle blond; magnums smashed
on the good ship abstinence
Scotland's fondness for whisky

crashed on the rocks
of the Temperance Act
no going back
drinking's only a problem when it's a problem
taken in reverse, there's no hiccup   no thirst

only I'm here, pint glass snow angel, washed up
in a Wetherspoons, where it's cheaper to drink
than at home or anywhere at all since the seventies
I seem to be half-in, half-out the kitchen
sopping   knowing
if I'm wearing this much drink
how much have I been drinking?

like a thrown voice
I can hear myself whimpering
prohibition
prohibition
prohibition

HAIKU INTERMISSION

MP3s suffice
as audio files, but don't
please audiophiles

saw him standing there
identical facial hair
beards of a feather

songs for minotaurs
mournful horns and minor chords
to reach it, amazed

IN AN OCTOPUS'S BETTING SYNDICATE UNDER THE SEA

in memory of Paul the octopus

never trust an octopus
to be impartial
they change colours
like an armchair fan
a marine Nostradamus
binary choices
there are underwater forces
depths where sharks circle
outstanding debts
and you sleep with the fishes
a feint to the home team – you bet away
sign your slip in deep black ink
in for a squid, as they say
the winner's been decided
in an octopus's betting syndicate under the sea
controlled by the tides, all else is theatre
noise and drama, waves that ripple
and pull you under
console yourself as you count out
the readies, it's an inside job
outcomes driven by gilled heavies
and a single, solemn nod
from the don of the cephalopods
sunken emperor
of the fixed odds

A THOUSAND DEAD CANARIES

finally you know
the small crunching sound
beneath your feet

to be the tiny shingle bodies
of a thousand dead canaries

their slight, songless forms
illuminated, captured
in a match head's
stuttering flame

tread carefully in the pitch
there are things
more bearable unlit

44,000 GRAMS OF PURE H2O

the maximum amount of liquid
allowed through airport security
in any one container
is 100 ml

I read this, already in line
acutely aware I am 60% water
and incapable of dispensing

I am unwittingly smuggling
44,000 grams of pure H2O

be cool, Ash
don't slosh

perspiration floods my forehead
like a swift incoming tide – good
that should lighten the load, I think
furtively sniffing telltale drops
of drink that school at my nostrils

my passport is something
caught by a trawlerman
laminated with barnacles
bound to my hand with kelp
it bears a likeness
of porpoise or kraken
when questioned
I will gurgle like a well

a businessman in front is pulled aside
personnel hunt for rubber gloves
contraband goods
beyond the metal detector
a security guard smugly juggles

the latest high-tech super plunger
a sudden surge – I'm going

under

a dam straining, I breach
airport security, ride
the unquenched thirst
through duty   free
staff shouting impotently
adrift on tobacco
capsized flotillas of toiletries
Krispy Kremes gripped as life rings
the departure lounge turns tsunami
luggage carousels swept out to sea
I'm spreading out to all four corners
beyond borders and checkpoints
orders and clipboards
fingers dabbling the surface
the gentle plop of pooh sticks
the soft/ serene/ acoustics

whatever the science
I always sensed we were solid
constituently more flesh than blood
a sturdy fish from mud, more
than the water left behind
but, like the earth, liquid overrides
press your ear to another
hear the lapping of the tides
come closer, no man is an island
no nation, left alone to skeleton
tributary digits waving
pulling near a new Pangaea

here, let us be as river and sea
overlap until I am you
and you are me – global, indivisible

to emerge – a circle of shining stars
vivid lighthouses in the boldest blue

TWO AND A HALF CHORDS

his rock 'n' roll ambitions stalled
at two and a half chords   never mind
the spirit he sought
came more in wrecking floors
bathroom stalls, devastation
met by apologetic label execs
blank cheques. unsigned, he couldn't afford the tariffs
public conveniences (conveniently) were fair game
clad in leather jacket, hair lacquered, air riffs
rock god – toss the mane, preen
beneath bog paper lasers, two-ply pyro show
amplified widescreen in mirrors cracked
dryers smacked in slow-mo. another nick in the wall
windmill-bash a tile then fall
to heroic knees, force faucets
then flee   before the paparazzi
              before the constabulary
arrive. fists held high
clutching sheaths
from abused machines, off
to find patch-jean cuties, groupies
adrenalised, afternoon writ large
in gutter headlines – the cash cow
of kowtowing magazines
the Kaiser of the Khazi
hell-raiser of the soft latrine

an APB sounds out for an urgent clean
an attendant arrives, surveys the scene
shrugs: an anachronism, hackneyed
as hurling a television   and her mind drifts
to a reformed Bucks Fizz
trashing a Starbucks pisser
Five Star turning a three-star
Centre Parcs bathroom one-star
she recalls Oasis blocking a sink   on purpose

when your career can disappear
with a squeegee and a mop
flushed away with the flotsam, dropped
a flash in the pan, a glitter ball cock

TWENTY-FIVE ON TWENTY-FIVE

I had the clearest picture/ followed my dreams like they were
scripture/ clarity to my narrative, a structure/ when people wrote
their wishlist wants/ I was ticking off accomplishments/ fifty things
to do before you die?/ I was twenty-five on twenty-five/ but vibrant
anecdotes water down/ wash out to war stories/ dog-eared antics of
former glories/ buried in a groove/ on the move but the axis never
shifts/ act—

unfold the map/ backpack that mothballed heart/ we used to take
pictures as an aide-memoire/ now we keep the world at arm's
length/ only photograph ourselves/ check the frame/ what have you
got?/ your fat head obscuring Angkor Wat?/ welcome to the pleasure
dome/ can't live in the moment – it must be owned/ recorded and
shown for *post*erity/ a tree falls in a forest and no one Instagrams it –
did it?/ I can't see the wood for the tweets

my life's essentially a pilot I've been trying for years to get greenlit/
its plot aimless, unrealistic/ its protagonist flawed, self-absorbed,
narcissistic/ it is a vehicle for me/ I am the in-on-it *Truman Show*/ and
through it I'll show True Man

what's on your mind?/ that I must post something at its most
relevant/ announce the death of someone eminent/ before the dam
breaks/ Prince died – along with the Wi-Fi/ finally online – tributes
from the world and its non-gender-specific life partner/ I must break
it first/ it's not enough to converse with friends/ at work/ with
neighbours/ I must holler it/ within finite characters/ to strangers

ever left your phone at home by mistake?/ hot hunger of not knowing
rising rampant in your face/ caught your thumb twitching confused,
a phantom limb/ pocket light as theft/ can't post what you had for
breakfast/ can't follow that link/ can't share your new 'do/ every
half-thought you think/ all that noise circulating through the wires –
and you're uncluttered/ isn't it glorious?

your neck muscles unknot / you're no longer looking down, you're looking up / you're spared *happy 9th wedding anniversary, babes, I love you lots* / posted by someone whose spouse / is at that moment sat next to them on the couch / you're not tempted to take / thirty-seven near-identical pictures of your own face / you're not overrun with the ins and outs of Brexit / the must-see boxsets / and 10,000 cat gifs / you have the gift of time – act / fifty things to do before you die? / a bucket list? / fuck it, it's now / who wants Venice for a rainy day? – you'll drown

SHADORMA INTERMISSION III

armed teachers
no dark sarcasm
punkstual
history
lessened? hands up, students – Miss
can use an Uzi

on Charles Bridge
selfie-stick tourists
frame themselves
paints idle
caricaturists look on
with oversized eyes

she said she
liked the way I smelt
I liked the
way she sniffed
me, breathed me deeply into
her body like myrrh

GOOD MORNING VITAMIN

my girlfriend is a DJ
on Superdrug's in-store radio station
her favourite artists are Shampoo
Cream
and Sandie Shaw   for Men

her between-song patter is a perky blend
of the facile   and subtle coaxing
to increase footfall
in the odour-eater aisle
hers is a podium for top pop
and Imodium. she is a purveyor
of classic tunes
and menthol Tunes. sales figures
spiking for condoms
following Marvin Gaye's 'Let's Get It On'
is her proudest moment to date
that, and her impromptu parody
'Let's Gaviscon'

her ultimate dream is to work at 6 Music
she sees this as a stepping stone
confident the way her career is headed
she'd nonetheless miss influencing
someone's facial contouring
and knowing her listeners got down
to Nicki Minaj as they got threaded

her trademark cry
of *Gooooood Morniiiiiiinnnnnggggg Vitamin!!!*
is a rallying call to store managers
and nail technicians alike

Superdrug Radio is a bubble
the outside world does not interrupt

the seamless shift from Ed Sheeran
to invisible deodorant sticks
Superdrug Radio does not report
on terrorist attacks
or constitutional crises
it does report on discounted self-adhesive dressings
it breaks it first. it is the place to be
for the latest releases
from Beyoncé   and Veet

my girlfriend places subliminal messaging
within the offers, subversion
in the suntan lotion promotion
easy access to Berocca
over-the-counter medicine
and sixties psychedelia
is a potent mix

she will tell you there's two-for-one
on all pills
load up
knock yourself out
here's The Moody Blues

when listeners call her dope
that meaning is manifold

she scooped the board
at the Pharmaceutical Radio Awards
taking home three gongs
including Best Afternoon Show
(narrowly beating out SemichemFM)
and Best Segue Into a Song –
for skin that's coarse and rough
try Nivea Dry Skin Lotion
and when the going gets tough
you can rely on Billy Ocean…

a boundary-pusher
increasingly audacious
in her audio playlists
she claims to have alerted
Superdrug shoppers first
to the latest trends in Albanian
thrash-grime. she's choice

queen of the decks
for Latin lovers with dry lips
hairy pecs and waxing strips
oozing charm, oozing hits
strongarm tactics for super-dry armpits
slipped disc? she'll slip your favourite disc
into her playlist. she's the cure for your illness
wake up to Pink and pinkeye eyedrops
break-out and make-up
at the hottest club
on the high street
she's DJ Dr Feelgood
she's superfly
she's Superdrug

THIS POEM

this poem has been subjected to rigorous focus group testing
its vowel sounds rolled around the mouth
of an influential tween from Preston
shared with her 3.5 million YouTube subscribers
like slavering dogs, all parties court its allegiance
this first stanza – teased-out – didn't break the internet
it mullered it. it is clickbait, viral meme, it is adman dream

this poem has been papped and snapped, it has trended –
a source close to the poem disclosed to the *Standard*
it partied with two of *Thingamajig's* kids Thursday night
then left *The Club* with a noted socialite. tongues wagged
they disappeared in a cab, all eyes on the metre

yes, *Celebrity News*reader, call it *free, post-commodity*
overuse the word *super* as an adverb
hail it the one true thing that exists anymore
something real, pure. recognise in it
your jaded idealism, those wasted years
of journalism, stray (before the film begins again)
from the autocue to scream how we're all one
inauspicious endorsement from ubiquity, all we love
pawned to the highest bidder, sold back at twice the price
thrice the speed, half the feel, done up like a dog's dinner
touch the goosebumps – they're bullets on your arm
blink back the prickling tears as your eyes – overcome – fill
recompose, fix rictus grin, look meaningfully into the lens – and
            announce
'now back to Steven Seagal, in *Driven to Kill*'

AN AMERICAN BEER COMPANY PRESENTS:
THE ROYAL MILE

I live on a street on which nobody lives
tenements purged of permanent tenants
aired out to Americans
investigating some distant Campbell
my neighbours change daily
residential displacement is good for the economy
key boxes and entry codes
are the trappings of home
this street is a replica, here for your pleasure
tarted up, tartaned out, set in haggised aspic
all that glitters is most certainly not Gold

you know the walkways and closes
you've been led down the rabbit hole
by drama students – all deadeye focus
and ostentatious cape fixations
walking tours, ghosts tours, golf tours
top hats and plus-fours
little Hitlers with follow-me flags
the bright yellow buses that shuttle by my window
if you look to your left, there's a poet
in his dressing gown at lunchtime eating soup
I'm your colourful slice of Edinburgh life
bringing flavour and authenticity

have you done the deep-fried-Mars Bar-eating experience yet?
the whisky-drinking experience?
you simply can't go another step
without a fluffy Nessie
shoved into your must-have
I ♥ *Edinburgh* sporran
everyone wears a kilt round here
to not do so is to stand out
ours is a climate in which to bare your knees

we have so much money
and so much time
                      and we're everywhere
retirement lasts fifty years
adolescence forever
put on your waterproofs
and beat a well-worn path
take a selfie in front of a red letterbox
eat some fudge, attempt a Scottish accent –
the locals love that. visit one of the many shops
where it really is Christmas every day
then reboard the bus
and if you think it's busy in May
just wait 'til August

have you been on the street
beneath the street yet?
it's just like the times of Black Death
only the actors die every hour
spend your strange money at the gift shop
remember your visit with a small picture
of a narrow walkway on an eraser
then reboard the bus

the next time you rub something out
think of us

MY GIRL, THE WASP TORMENTOR

my girl torments wasps
it's what she's always done. observe
the instinctive way
she riles one, the slender brutality
skilled hand pestering
unwitting prey, here
are innate mechanics at play. hear

the sickening shift in pitch
the spiralling intensity –
travel hairdryer to buzzsaw
a trapped insect's sound
and fury, as she feints
and dips, the tanda, the citar
– olé, micro-matador!
a million bastard things taunted
only four career stings

seldom do I see her
straighten her back
sharp glint in that ocular glass
sense the temperature change
the walls sweat and contract
I know then there is a foe
in the room worthy of the name
her A-game. such contests may last hours
combatants exhausted, sapped
of powers. I've known her
to respectfully bow, open a window
declare a draw; buzz-drunk
the wasp swoons, wheezes   paraglides
to revive on the breeze

she talks of ringing the legs
of her toughest opponents

some nights in her sleep
she reenacts highlights

often after a mammoth battle
something primal in her needs   now
those torturous panther pads paw
for mine – make contact; here, supine
on the settee, we entwine   but her kisses
are gum, a flavourless lick of endorphins
in each diminishing one, dopamine
exiting her body like sportsman spit
I'm not so much provoked as present
a boy forlornly running
to meet a retreating tide

I hum softly near her ear – to trick hard-wiring
something flickers, a cave painting
lit yellow on black walls. I wait
for the hands to dance, her guard
to rise and fall, wait for the swat
hot and heavy, to score my flesh
a band of stripes to brand my back

she said once she didn't understand wasps
'what creature hurts for fun?'
her eyes black as a burned-out star
I stared out the standard lamp
bit down hard on my tongue
until my tongue stung

BOWL CUT

as a cost-cutting exercise, my dad
would use a pudding bowl to trim
the hair of my youth; there was no grace
no élan, in the shape or scissoring
it was a job to consume minimum
man hours, be done before Mum
needed the kitchen table and, though executed
lickety-split, be undertaken with sufficient care
to ensure not a single white-blond hair
should tumble into rhubarb crumble
or contaminate the Saturday bake
– and if the bowl was needed for a cake
my haircut must wait

it was when Dad was laid off
things began to change. he was not a man
who handled inactivity well. my hair
became a fascination – a way to release
pent-up boredom, stoke his imagination
I didn't mind the rabbit jelly mould
my hair set really well in that thing
friends, none of whose coiffure
resembled a woodland creature
crowded round in awe, deeply impressed
        (the gravy boat was less of a success)

his eyes would roam each room
weighing up options – ashtrays
lampshades, serrated tools
when he wasn't scanning the house
he would stare at my head
with the impatience of a farmer
hamstrung by a relentless winter

I'd accompany him on trips
to antiques shops   stand respectful

and mortified   as various items were tried
atop my bonce, customers askance
full of pity for whatever avant-garde
monstrosity I already sported

the odder the object's shape, the more certain
it was to be bought. several times he decimated
the shopping budget – the ceramic vase
with curled waves that gave me a nautical look
think Poseidon: The Teenage Years
a mighty tide tucked behind
the seawall of my ears

my school photos were legendary
it wasn't until deep into secondary
I was ever symmetrical
mine were the only shots sold
outside the family circle
Edward Scissorhands opening
nearly broke me – the parallel topiary
I'd been cut by a monster, misunderstood
ostracised by my follicles

eventually, of course, you outgrow
the parental influence. peer pressure
a sense of cool, money from a paper round
an awareness of culture, then counter-culture
I went it alone – new romantic, greb
the Rachel, Rolling Stone

on mantlepieces at my parents' home
decommissioned artefacts warped, cracked
streaked auburn with rust, tarnished vases
flaunted vast afros of dust

confronting again those accursed basins
the day my father turned eighty
surrounded by family and old mining buddies

he unwrapped a bowl my wife and I found
in a junk shop in Germany. placing
his trusty old rusted scissors
in those faltering arthritic fingers
I took a chair. do your worst, I laughed
slipping off my suit jacket

the linoleum banked, avalanched
under blizzards of hair, a snow globe
shook by shaking hands
time and place fell away

when the massacre was done
I sported three hairstyles – or none
part loo brush, part voodoo doll
part shunned chimp
it was his masterpiece. I returned

the scissors to the mantelpiece
each man at peace, stunned into reverie

it will grow out, I thought, with some sadness
touching a skull that with each passing year
more and more resembled his

NONET INTERMISSION III

nominative determinism
led to Fred Couples Counselling
quit the clubs – advice pitched to
partners playing away
reconciled through rough
times, wedges healed
TLC
to a
tee

loaned to the deep, the seabed, my son
dive down in your sleep, far below
the pillow, your ocean. roll
afishionado
like sharks, never still
between worlds, gills
wide. we wait
for your
wake

NO GOOD AT ACCENTS

I'm no good at accents
                    I can't even do my own
something akin to the slapping sound
a shoe makes when its sole works
loose. this is one I have cultivated
to seem more cultured

I envy those parochial poets
proudly evoking home in vocal tones
honed in close-knit neighbourhoods
high-density zones – the legitimacy
of a meaningful street, a tree
that means something
different to everyone in the room –
hid in it, fell out of it, kissed under it
campaigned for its protection; I see it
leaf and shed in each oak-soaked vowel

I have my parts of many towns
preferred routes, favoured dives
can hear the crackling lure of old 45s
I may have seen a band there
quite possibly done a gig
but this isn't my city
my consonants don't drip
with its marketplace and arcades
there is no history in my cadence
I don't instinctively know to ask
for barm or bap, cob or roll
besides, my pronunciation of each
may require a repeat
I lack those local flourishes
the little provincial in-jokes
that buddy strangers

my voice is mongrel, doggerel, magpie, thief
borrowed nuances, stolen speech
true place beyond tongue's reach
no trees line this neighbourhood
I am gangplank, I am driftwood

POMMEL TAPIR

a pommel horse?
more like a pommel tapir
the way its snout tapers
a disapproving frown
stitched down its suede
that critic's nose – snorting, haughty
dismayed: another four-point-nought
another dismount falling short
a convoy of buckling legs, unsteady toes

around five the janitor
locks the gym
all that's falling
now, tumbles of dust
and the night

spotlit in lunar light
pommel tapir stretches
stiff haunches, flexes back
launches into the perfect handspring
enacts front tuck, a walkover

tomorrow it's the turn
of the youngest class
knees knots in cotton
syrupy grasps
newborn foals
graceless and wonky
lifted onto pommel tapir
as onto a seaside donkey

too little to see the gym
for what it is tonight
scorecards held high
in a unison of tens
and a flood of tears
that flow across the floor
like a sea of thrown flowers

I WASN'T BORN

I wasn't born, I was launched
nine months of trials at the test centre
teased out, emerging through smoke, a torch
passed, copper wire placenta

cord cut by three profs
with brilliant white blazers
and a flair for spectacle. shown off
atop a pedestal, acclaimed by lasers

and loud generic rock. I am the apex
my data calibrated, forefront spec
state of the artist, the very latest
add-ons and graphics. hi-tech

graphite and cobalt. applauded
into being. what it is to be invincible
unquestioning and gleaming. awarded
life, under eternal guarantee. convinced

of one's own immortality. you scale trees
drop, not knowing what it is to fall. get up again
bounce around the playground, scuff steel knees
wipe down chrome. uncracked. pain

is not yet written into your programming
sheltered by non-experience, factory-set
an *algorithm for impeccable living*
you are impervious. secure. protect-

ed by the hard shell of the family unit
                yet all too soon it seems
links are tested, wires loose, decrepit
there are glitches in the machines

what doesn't kill you
kills part of you

pressured to plug in to a cold system
made bloodless by boxes, made product
controlled and cajoled – keep up, anachronism
your tinnitus dial tone, your tarnished chrome, there's rust

in your adamantium. I once was Christ
spun the world on my dominant hand
a market leader, I was zeitgeist
top price, I was high-demand

beware – younger, fitter
products are everywhere. airbrushed
further, fillers and filters
I'm analogue – halted, shushed

told to call out to our appliances
like they're real, to politely use a branded given name
so agreeable and compliant, in thrall to the science
believe their indispensability   and fall away

nought in the manual about gears turning flesh
fresh air expanding iron lungs
voluntary movements bloom in my cortex
strange portents – I'm speaking in tongues

I cut with ease, all the deaths I have known
crawl in, overpower elementary system
I try my defibrillated heart – it starts on its own
something organic pumping discs and pistons

offline, I pine for nature, and nature comes
the latest downgrade goes by unclicked
siren screens scream in retreat, shunned
I hum their weakening beat, boned of bowers, bunting, brick

from light particle to unfinished article
in art as in life: a draft, a drawing, raw and sketchy
rebooted human, open and vulnerable
welcome, weakness, you incomplete me

UNFREE VERSE

forced to write poetry
as part of a new community service initiative
don't do the crime
if you can't do the rhyme
we're often reminded (supervisor humour)

form apportioned, punishment
proportional to the gravity of the felony
shoplifting, trespassing, minor first-time offences
served in haiku or limerick, non-custodial sentences
pencilled under house supervision

public intoxication
schlepped off in a drunk tanka

for those falling
a hair's breadth short of prison –
for the hard-boiled villain: the villanelle
Tang. to see someone sweat and struggle, curse hell
stress over syllables, is to witness justice first-hand (and second)

a study in length and time. structure imposed
(suppress the great I Am). there is no free verse
chain-ganged, shackled feet, restraints, constraints
in a musty library under minimum security
we seek pastoral intervention

in the right line
lieth rehabilitation

oh, poetry – my keeper! my rescuer! in its bloody rigour
I am honest   vandalism? panhandleism?
trivial offences, the first sly sightlines of prison
career thieves seized on plagiarism
I found the straight, the narrow

a facility for correction and form
character after character reformed
rewritten   reborn
clean sheet

                              new leaf

RADIO EMO

you're listening to the breakfast show
on Radio Emo

for those who like their cereal
funereal

AMERICANA

it might be rebranded Americana
but I carry scars of steel guitars
fiddles are anxiety triggers
back to Damoclesian cassettes we reeled
from, shivered and sniggered
the middle-aged women in pigtails and gingham
serenading through straw men like their pa
cob-piped, combovered, slack-jawed

tonight, the mosh pit is floored, unstuck
no spit and sawdust – transformed
by cabaret seating, transatlantic stardust
two plaintive songs have come
and gone, politely received
tables, ours youngest here by a decade
where am I among the grey and decayed?
southern France or Spain or somewhere
on a long car journey, in the back seat
with my brother, black leatherette fizzing
in summer heat. we pick up the underside
of frying thighs, alternately
like the scalded desert feet
of little lizards

before the first of many wrong turns
holiday mood unspooling on back roads
the Reader's Digest guides
are sought: the Master Tapes
the back cover a roster of improbable names –
Dolly and Merle. Hank. Telecasters – woozy
and nasal, vocal inflections like sagged elastic
Craig and I liked 'A Boy Named Sue'
but that was a comedy number
in short supply among the jezebels
and good ol' folk, archetypes and tropes

we wanted Whitesnake and 'Paradise City'
but got 'Love Is Like a Butterfly'
and whatever was Conway Twitty

I bought both artists' new releases
lined up, got them signed
back at the flat, I play a first side
the gap between my father's tastes
and mine narrowing further with every spin
something in that sound – elegiac, timeless –
has me in shorts again in that old Ford
four-minute soap operas score
strange straight roads
intractable lives, the battle lines
of drink and fidelity, honest toil
universal truths scorched in soil
settled in the petrichor. I can see
a little way beyond the door, beyond
the window, there's a world
for which I'm being prepared

the cassette pauses confession
somewhere near or not near Carcassonne
misdirection calls for maps and hush
in the back, ghosts; shrouds of songs echo
in the airlessness. I know these sounds
loss and longing, mournful tones
I don't need anyone to press a button
to bear the bittersweet heft of love. I hear you
and will always hear you. familiar strains
are calling me home

SHADORMA INTERMISSION IV

more tigers
in US than wild
kept as pets
caged, distressed
they long for long grass, freedom
as they're fed Frosties

for virus
try disinfectant
inject it
into veins
suggests vain ineffective
reject president

best pop group
with a veg-themed name
he said, is
Prefab Sprout
singularly forgetting
Pak Choi Division

FRESHERS' WEEK

ten years ago:
descending as much to teach as learn
they swarm the streets, enquiring minds blasted
to bits – salvos of two-for-one shots, indomitable
youth, plucked from the sticks, from apron strings.
proof is in the pudding and it's jelly (40%)
roaming, fresh-packed, tall, broad-backed, hell-sent
turning the city centre smoke-black, erasing all history
        to the indigenous, Biff Tannen
has stolen a sports almanac, set fire to wheelie bins
stoked revolution. we are not the coming generation
we are the now – and we intend to come
tonight. liberty slips from short skirts, hips and tits
to make you cry; hormones unbottled from lips
every abetting phone, every vaped face there to be kissed
or punched; they swagger, stagger and scream
steaming, brimming with capers, Rizla papers
it's Sodom and Gomorrah with a Yates's
this is not my city, but it will be, baby
maybe before this night is out – I have seen the future
and vomited on its shoes, I have cried hallelujah
into the leathery neck-folds of an outnumbered bouncer
autographed Old Big Head's midriff in pedigree piss
I have left my mind and heart on Parliament Street
drunk until I cannot stand, until I cannot speak
then gone for a kebab. step aside
your leaders are here, your innovators
the grand debaters, swaying down your street
a first play for greatness this freshers' week

today:
we're fresher
free of that term, sober
is the new shitfaced
glasses raised to the cafés
raising hell is passé, pass
my turmeric latte.   please

FENLAND INFIDELITY

receipts are extraneous
shove them into pockets
and forget about them
that meal for two, that double room

                                where were you, my love?
it'll all come out in the wash

a tired Fenland hotel, an off-season rate
a fictitious seminar in Harrogate
       I'll wait
revenge is a dish best served
with your fucking awful potatoes

A CORVID AUDIENCE

you catch your name, misspelt
in the venue window
next to a photo
of David Dickinson
and all that preshow bravado
a febrile farrago
is gone, pronto. how feeble the artistic ego
how quickly butterflies
transmogrify into vultures
unpicked sutures
I foresaw tables of soon-to-be
devasted nonagenarians
a vengeful Nantiques Roadshow
the banner above the photo
read: *A Crow-Pleasing Cabaret!!!!*
amateur night at the ol' Dog and Duck

I've played some trying rooms –
toddlers, paralytic misanthropes
Young Conservatives –
even so, this was a shock
something out of Hitchcock, inside
stout and sable, crowded round tables
were rows and rows
of crows
feathers on seats as far as the lights reached
on last, vital time to rethink an approach –
what would fly with a corvid audience?

the compère did mostly jackdaw jokes
the mothers-in-law of the seventies
velour-suited club comic. example:
why did the jackdaw cross the road?
– because they're insanely inquisitive!
(if you think this is in any way funny, imagine being a crow – it slayed

94

if not, well, it's not meant for you)

first up proper, a piece of physical theatre, schlock horror
man in scarecrow garb, cruciform arms, stick up his arse
still as an egg, as the room's expressions
this might have frightened had they yet to fledge
wet behind the beak, still in the nest
but this generation grew up watching *Saw*
how could they not be bored by an idiot made straw?

crows aren't finches
you can't affix a bell to a stick
knowing they'll be entertained for hours
a magician, a mime, a folk singer came
and went, dispatched to a clapless restlessness

you could've powered a small town
on the nervous energy in the green room
before the start – the walls juddered, the floor
with swift indecency, it housed the fallout of war
each turn returning torn apart, punch-drunk
keen to drink more heavily than before
each failure adding an extra layer
to the next performer, until
swamped in bloody furs
they could no longer function
or recall a bloody word

        only a thought had occurred
I once performed to a hen party
of actual hens
sure, the set wasn't wholly transferrable
it was mostly about laying (they clucking loved the innuendo)
but this, and the pharmaceutical rider, had given me confidence
why had I only now remembered this?

also that I once accompanied Lou Reed
in a reading of Poe's 'The Raven' to a select audience

of ravens, or that I recited a series of sonnets
from a reedbed hide to a siege of bitterns
that no less an authority than Chris Packham
described as *titillating*

the crow show set went ok, as it happens
challenging crowd, though, for a non-birder
toughest gig outside of Glasgow   murder

FOX FISHING

have you ever gone fishing
for a fox? baited a line
with a chicken neck, cast it out
into the buddleia and bracken
that swarm the railway tracks
Beeching's gift to nature

not here to harm one   but marvel at it
dare-dream fingers to muss sunburst fur
as though a new lover's hair, have its eyes
meet mine, implicitly know
not all flesh is foe

an angler might tell you it's the getaway
the calm   *but my little heart beat so fast*
a rustle in the underbrush
a starling unearthing, a thrush
but I'm imagining
bosky paths parting
a lone streetlight's
watery orange glare
a lone streetfighter's
wary orange stare
hue of a life vest
of a solar flare

I was four and four months
when a fox burst
into my bedroom
through a window left open
all summer until then
I tried to shout for Mum
but only my eyes screamed
the fox, stunned likewise, froze
an unpinned grenade on my bed

its environment transposed
Star Wars figures and football posters
its brush – bushy, unearthly –
laid out across Charger, my toy rhino

                  and best friend

there are things communicated
intrinsic truths passed in the flash
of an unseeing eye. connections
that can't be explained
or verbalised, when you understand
you are but an organism. whatever tech
all that white noise insists we need   pitched to us!
us of tissue and bark and stubborn weed!
of fur and fin and brackish bleed!

those times you think you dream
your life. that it's out by the tracks
the trees, the leaves, yours
to inhale – the very earth
to pause and breathe out
mulch and musk, den and dirt

I never knew this as woods
snarled and gnarly, dense as chemo
before the neat rows of produce goods
grassy banks bulldozed for show homes
the few spared trees – pollarded, beheaded –
by which I glide, blood of beast, agrestal-boned
I multiply in my mind, until I'm stood
face-to-face with lynx, wolf, with bear
there be dragons here

a tentative tug, lightning
down the line   then nothing   a pounding of silence
before a second fierce bite pulls the rod down
my heart yelping, breath short
feet, braced, planted in the earth
I pull the tip up, begin to reel in
this isn't a fishing rod, it's a timeline

the wind drops away to a soundless lull
just a thin line separating us as animals
something real, something beautiful
just beyond those trees   at the right angle

DIARIES: INSTRUCTIONS FOR OUTLAWS

Over a period of three years our intrepid team of cameramen endeavoured to film the elusive poet Ash Dickinson engaged in writing his third collection, *Instructions for Outlaws*.

Camping out in often arduous terrain, buffeted by the elements, lenses fruitlessly focused on deserted laptops and journals, lead cameraman Mike DePenske, with over twenty years' experience of filming poets in the wild, sensed early on this was to be a test of patience and resolve. 'Many poets have routines, they begin writing at 7am, clock off at 2pm – all you need do is set up the equipment. You could've launched a rocket by Maya Angelou.' Within days it became apparent Dickinson was no such poet.

DePenske and his assistant, Steed Gellinger, frustrated by hours and hours of Dickinson doing little more than watching Netflix and staring off into space, decided to set up remote camera traps. 'We'd not seen our families in six weeks and had, at best, only a few useable seconds of him absentmindedly moving one word back and forth while fiddling with his hair. I'd missed my daughter's sixth birthday. We were frazzled. Morale was at a low ebb.'

Fitted with a motion sensor and night vision, these cameras were able to record the precise moment Dickinson began 'Hipsters Ruined Beards'. 'Swaying into shot, a punctured windsock in flares, clearly in from some bar or other, he began bashing away at the keys as though they were a piñata of money. The energy and dementedness of that moment was electrifying to behold.' There followed an amazing sequence in which they captured Dickinson writing what became, practically verbatim, the third stanza, before he disappeared behind the sofa, remaining there for the next ten hours with just his shoes peeking out. DePenske and Gellinger, reviewing this footage the next day, were beside themselves: 'It felt like a significant breakthrough but, as always with night vision, the film was grainy, and reluctantly we had to conclude it would only be of secondary use.'

Nonetheless, the team returned to their task revitalised. All too often, though, Dickinson would appear, open a Word document, pull a face, then dissolve back into the tundra, into that rockface of LPs, just another shadow among the wooden flooring and overhanging shelves of paperbacks. 'Several times we'd see him, hurriedly set our cameras up to record, only for him to vanish again just as quickly. Our editor rang daily for the rushes and often the best we could do was send blurry pictures of a retreating back.'

Months passed with barely even a sighting. Gellinger got sick, feverish. DePenske, despite his lengthy experience in the field, began to suffer hallucinations, at one point believing himself to be the reincarnation of Anne Boleyn. On one grim October day, he went over seven hours without blinking.

Their patience was eventually rewarded, some two and a half years into the project, by Dickinson's growing awareness of the passing of time and a rocketing self-imposed deadline. 'We started to get some very useable footage. My wife had left me by this point, taking the kids, and Steed was a full-blown alcoholic, communicating mainly in the low howl of an abused dog, but the poems were coming.

'I haven't signed on for book four.'

Lightning Source UK Ltd.
Milton Keynes UK
UKHW012005060922
408432UK00003B/797

9 781913 958237